James Ewing Ritchie

Imperialism in South Africa

James Ewing Ritchie

Imperialism in South Africa

ISBN/EAN: 9783744752480

Printed in Europe, USA, Canada, Australia, Japan

Cover: Foto ©ninafisch / pixelio.de

More available books at **www.hansebooks.com**

IMPERIALISM

IN

SOUTH AFRICA.

BY

J. EWING RITCHIE,

Author of " The Night Side of London," " Days and Nights in London,"
" On the Track of the Pilgrim Fathers," " British Senators," &c.

SECOND EDITION, REVISED, CORRECTED, AND ENLARGED.

London :

JAMES CLARKE & CO., 13 & 14, FLEET STREET

1881.

Price One Shilling.

CONTENTS.

CHAPTER I.

INTRODUCTION.

THE following papers were written before in England we had begun to think much about the Boers, when we were preparing to crush Cetewayo and his people, and when the general opinion appeared to be that it was a great and blessed work to promote Christianity and civilisation by shooting down the uncivilised and heathen Kaffirs—that is, such as our traders had not killed off with Cape smoke, the most infamous liquor under the sun. We succeeded. We crushed the Zulus, and, flushed with glory—that peculiar glory which results from a strong man knocking down a weak one—our gallant troops returned home, leaving behind them desolation and death. The bill of costs was rather heavy, but that is paid, not by the men who make the wars, nor by the men who are so ready to fight in them, but chiefly by poor writers like myself, farmers ruined by bad weather and American competition, small shopkeepers, clerks with limited incomes and unlimited families, country parsons who find it exceedingly difficult to bring up their children in the way of life in which Providence has been pleased to place them, widows who have known better days, and that enormous section of the middle class who in these happy times find themselves being ground to dust like wheat in a flour-mill, between the British artizan on one side and the great capitalist on the other, and who cling to what they call respectability as passionately as any ancient spinster to the love *souvenirs* of a gay and giddy youth. It is upon these and such as these falls the burden of a glory of which they know nothing but the cost. Of course I pleaded in vain. The public opinion of the colonists in South Africa was in favour of war, as it always is; war to give them more land, their sorest need, seeing that every acre of the country is already in the hands of large proprietors; and Sir Bartle Frere was known to be a godly man. Even I have heard him make speeches at Exeter Hall.

Sir Bartle Frere was recalled, but the lust of Imperialism to which he had pandered, and of which he was such an admirable representative, remained. The colonists, eager for the fray, commenced the Basuto war, and at length our own authorities in the Transvaal forced matters to such a pass that the Boers had to rise against British injustice and British rapacity. Like their grand old fathers, who saved Holland from a Spain quite as Christian and almost as merciful as the England of to-day, and who in doing so saved Protestant England, shortly to build up across the Atlantic the greatest Republic the world has ever seen— these men, their descendants, ask themselves, as all true men do—

> " How can man die better
> Than facing fearful odds,
> For the ashes of his fathers
> And the temples of his gods? "

A scornful laugh was the reply of England to their mild protest. Who were the Boers, and how could they fight? asked the gentlemen of the Press, and all sections of what is called society. Well, the Boers have pretty well answered that question. At Laing's Nek and at Majuba Hill they have shown us what they can do. Better still, they have shown us what they are by their kindness to our wounded on the field of battle. The question comes, What are we to do? If the Transvaal was a great country like America, the answer would be, Submit the matter to arbitration; and if we did we should hear much in that stately and sonorous language, of which Mr. Gladstone is such a master, of the awful mischief that would have been occasioned by a war between England and America, and the newspapers, especially the Nonconformist section, would have eulogised him as the Saviour of his country. But, alas! the Boers are few. We have some thirteen thousand of our finest soldiers armed in the costliest and most effective

manner, ready and eager to fight, and thus, as we are in
the proportion of two to one, the cry is still, Forward, to
reap a glorious revenge! It is too late, we are told,
now to negotiate. It is too late now to listen to the
voice of reason. It is too late now to quit ourselves like
men. Our savage instincts are to be gratified at whatever cost. The Boers, with their wives and little ones, are
to be shot down. Their pleasant farms are to be laid
waste; their flocks are to be stolen, and their fields to be
left untilled. The British flag, which has braved a thousand years the battle and the breeze, will float proudly as
of yore, and under it the British gin dealer will open his
store, and sit happy and serene. The Boers, such as sur-
vive the slaughter, will once more have "trekked" out into
the desert. Their kindred in the Orange Free State, at the
Cape, or in Natal, will be more incensed against us than
ever, the difficulties of our rule will have been immensely
increased, and in the face of Europe and at the Bar of
Justice we shall stand condemned. How much better
would it be to retrace our steps, to admit that we have
been wrong from the first. Why cannot we do so? We
applaud the criminal who gives up crime, the thief
who takes to honesty. In heaven, we are told, there is
joy over one sinner that repenteth, but now when mercy
pleads and justice commands our reply is, As we have
begun so we must continue to the bitter end. To do
right now is to confess our fault. If we had beaten the
Boers we might have listened to them, as they came on
bended knees to sue for peace. Now that they have beaten
us we cannot sheathe the sword till we have shown them
that England is as unmerciful as she is unjust.

Alas! the Boers have few friends. They are simply
Republican farmers, anxious mainly to increase their
flocks, and to live on the soil they and their fathers have
cultivated and reclaimed. In the high places of the earth
they are little thought of, and their representatives are not
to be met with in European Courts. Lords and ladies
turn up their nose at their simple habits, condemn their want
of style, and imply that amongst them there is but a limited

use of soap and water. Bishops and archbishops have enough to do with their troublesome clergy, to exclaim against a policy which has driven the Bible-reading Boer to take up arms ; nor would they, if they could, as the army and the navy and the Church are but part and parcel of a system which our ruling classes consider as the glory of the land, and the wonder of surrounding nations. But why are the Dissenting ministers dumb ?—the men who may be said to be the leaders of that section of modern England which helped to put down slavery ; to abolish the Corn Laws ; to promote Free Trade, and to which the Liberal Party owes it that it is now at length revelling in place and power? Have they no word of protest now that we are preparing for a final massacre ? In these days of culture and refinement have they forgot the manly virtues of their fathers, who faced exile and imprisonment and poverty and death? I am told that they preach a broader Gospel. Is it that in their new Gospel they learn that it is Philistine to stand up for the oppressed? To lift up a voice on behalf of the weak? If so, we need not wonder when they complain that they cannot get the working man to come and hear them preach. He has many faults, I own ; nor do I regard him with a very reverent eye ; but there is this to be said of him, and that is much—that he has no faith in shams ; that he is the friend of an oppressed people, and that he likes to see fair play. If the question were to be settled by him, the soil of the Transvaal would be yet free of the blood of the slain. The men who met at the Memorial Hall the other day to bid England stay her hand were working men. The crowd who clustered round General Roberts, as he left to shoot down the Boers, last week, were solely the Upper Ten. In the long run, the working man is a better judge of what is right in politics than his master. Mr. Gladstone, at any rate, admits that he is a man and a brother.

With a heavy heart and almost in despair, I appeal to the public that this wickedness may be removed from our shoulders. If Mr. Gladstone had been in Opposition how eloquently he would have pleaded for the independence of the Transvaal. If Mr. Bright had been out of office how the world would have re-echoed with his invective. Even Mr. Courtney has not a word to say. The oracles are dumb.

"Apollo from his shrine
Can no more divine
With hollow shriek the steep of Delphos leaving."

Nevertheless, the truth will out, and from the distant Transvaal the cry echoes across the waves with redoubled and redoubling force. What can, for instance, be more touching than the letter of Field Cornet Pretorious to Colonel Lanyon in December, 1880, on the subject of probable hostilities.. Cornet Pretorious has a claim to be listened to, as he had at times incurred the displeasure of the Boers by establishing a corps of Transvaal Volunteers in the service of the Government. "I deem it my earnest duty," he writes to the Colonel, "to inform you, and at the same time to warn you against dreadful and fatal consequences which will rest on my shoulders and yours. I say, again, I have deceived myself, and I hope further your Excellency to think that the burghers, the protesting people, do not mean, or take to heart, their cause, aye, their just cause. I can tell you that if the Government intends not otherwise than has been hitherto made known to me, that we then will have to bear heavy and sad consequences. Believe me, your Excellency, I see torrents of blood and tears. Blood from the veins of the men, and bitter tears from the eyes of the women and children. The women and children will lament the loss of their husbands and fathers; they will weep, the children for bread, the mothers because they cannot give the bread, and, finally, they will weep because they have become foreigners in their own land. My hope and wish is that God will say to England: Until here, and no farther! But, Sir, think and consider that one innocent drop of blood will cry vengeance over the leader. Aye, you excuse yourself, and you accuse me and others that we shall be the cause of sad consequences. I will accuse you of having shed blood unjustly, aye, I feel my case so just that I almost venture to say that the blood of the men, whether

A 3

of the burghers or of the soldiers, will summon those that
have brought about and maintained the annexation before
the Throne of Judgment hereafter of the Judge of all. Or
do we not dread the Day of Judgment! I say : I dread, for
I believe in the Supreme Being. Sir, I am born under fire
in Natal when my father fought the English along with
the Boers ; hence, when I got my sense, I was a free Republican. The whole history of this country is known to
me, and, therefore, I venture to say that we have been
wronged on the 12th April, 1877. England has been
deceived by those who wrought the annexation, and we have
been deceived and misled by our head and our headmen,
because we have obeyed them to remain quiet. We have
thought that England's people would withdraw the arbitrary
annexation."

In spite of its uncouth English, what depth of feeling
there is in this brave Boer's letter, and how guilty are we,
the English people. I need not potter over Blue Books.
I need not weary the reader with official despatches. It
is sheer waste of time to study the sophistries of Sir
Bartle Frere. I need not quote even Mr. Gladstone's
condemnation of Lord Beaconsfield's Government for the
annexation of the Transvaal. We all know that the Boers
were annexed against their leave ; that they have appealed
to the English Cabinet, and to an English Queen in vain
for their rights ; and that if ever there was a righteous war
it is that in which the Boers are now engaged.

Let me take ground more in accordance with the trading
instincts of the community. When we talk about morality
and right, we are apt to get into a fog, and to use words
which have no meaning ; but pounds, shillings, and pence
are things we can all understand. When men talk about
their principles it is well to suspect, and ask them
what they mean; but figures are clear. It appears
from the recently-issued report of the Comptroller and
Auditor-General :—" The revenue of the Transvaal in 1879
was £93,408, and the expenditure £177,595 ;" that is to
say, the income was not much more than half the outlay.
In the same year the excess of liabilities over assets is,

in round numbers, £420,000. On financial grounds, at least, the Transvaal, as the *Pall Mall Gazette* remarks, does not seem to be worth the enormous outlay which its conquest will cost at once, and its retention will cost in perpetuity.

Again, there is another consideration. An American writer—Mr. Sticknay—arguing on behalf of economical Governments, says that the time is coming when a million of extra taxation may so cripple the American producer that he may be undersold in the markets of the world. If in America, with its energetic population, and its undeveloped resources, such a plea may be urged, how much stronger must it be in our case ? We are a trading people, and to undersell our competitors we must be able to produce more cheaply. Heavy taxation is quite inconsistent with cheap production. To realise the dream of Imperialism in South Africa we must have increased taxation, which means a bonus to our foreign competitor, while already, as every merchant and manufacturer knows, he is doing us enough mischief. This is impolitic, to say the least. It is said, further, that our commerce is declining, that there is a falling off in our foreign trade ; and no wonder—the more we spend in war the less money we have, and the less we shall continue to have. There is no expenditure more unprofitable than that of war. In Europe, at any rate, of the plagues that walk the earth there is none so full of evil influence on the world.

One other reason why the Boers should be left to themselves is the utter inability of England to rule them aright. Mr. Gladstone has complained in one of his political essays that the English Parliament is overloaded, that it has far more work than it can accomplish ; India excites little attention, and South Africa less. A colonial paper thus describes (1 quote the *Kaffrarian Watchman* of January 28) the utter ignorance of officers and statesmen at home where South Africa is concerned :—" History records that some years ago the question of appointing an extra chaplain to the troops then serving in South Africa was somewhat warmly opposed in the British Parliament, and one of the oppo-

nents to the appointment—His Grace of Argyll—sported his
knowledge of the geography of the colony by saying that
the chaplain then serving in South Africa could easily hold
morning service in Natal and preach to the troops in King
Williamstown the same evening ! It would appear that the
people who are determined to maintain themselves as rulers
over our internal affairs know no more of the topography of
the country than did the nobleman referred to when he made
his assertion some thirty years ago ; as, according to a Natal
paper, the commander of Her Majesty's steamer *Boadecia*,
now in Natal waters, received a recent cablegram to this
effect :—' Anchor off Potchefstroom, but do not shell the
town.' Can ignorance be more disgustingly pernicious to
the welfare and progress of a new country ? " Of course
not, and this is a very good reason why we should leave the
Boers alone.

Failing to govern the Boers from Downing Street, it
may be argued *à fortiori* the colonists at the Cape are
unequal to the task. In the Cape the colonists love to
talk of the Boers as brutes, because they keep out of the
way of the English and regard our countrymen—as they
have abundant reason to do—with dislike and suspicion.
They envy the Boer his fine climate and his productive
soil ; they despise his honest life and his simple aims. In
the *Kaffrarian Watchman*, which claims to be the Government organ of the district, I read, the other day, the
following lines, which may be accepted as a fair proof
that the mental calibre of the colonist is somewhat of the
lowest, and that his prejudices against the Boers quite unfit
him to give them fair play. What are we to think of a
people for whom an editor produces such wretched doggrel
as the following ?—

> Hurrah ! for England's equal rule,
>   Her rights she will maintain ;
> The Transvaal Boers will play the fool,
>   And half of them be slain.

> They make a boast about their rights,
>   And of their heroes true ;
> But bear in mind, my valiant knights,
>   John Bull is valiant too.

And if they once but rouse his ire,
  The Boers will flee apace,
It's then they'll find that England's fire
  'Ll exterminate their race.

As for Paul Kruger, who is he,
  Who dares our flag denounce?
A fool of the Transvaal he must be,
  Who'll burst with brag and bounce.

The cockney's the boy to teach him to plough;
  If he'd only be guided by him,
He could sit by his fireside with his old vrow,
  And enjoy his long pipe and his gin.

But no! the place where the brains ought to be
  Is unluckily stuffed full of leather;
But give the fools rope they'll haul it in free,
  And by-and-by get th' end of the tether.

It's then they will play a fresh tune on their fiddle,
  And sing, John Bull never roars
But when he's a mind with his horns to tickle,
  They'll shout out—Oh! spare us poor Boers.

And it's then poor old England, so brimful of mercy,
  Will teach our Dutch cousins to pray,
For all foolish rebels talk loud and saucy,
  To kneel down to John Bull and say—*Amen.*
                                        Jos. JONES.

Naturally we ask how can a community of which this gifted Jones is a fair specimen understand or appreciate the Boers? What chance have the latter of justice at the hands of the former when even a friend of the Boers is bespattered with mud and loaded with abuse, and regarded as a traitor and a miscreant? There was a time when it seemed possible that of their own free will the Boers might have come to terms with us, and have become part of that South African Confederation of which Lord Carnarvon and Mr. Froude were so much enamoured, and to promote which it was understood Mr. Gladstone, criminally, as it seems to most people, allowed Sir Bartle Frere to remain. But that dream has now no chance of becoming true—its realisation seems further off than ever. We have made enemies of the Boers, and the less England or the Cape interferes in their concerns the better in that part of the world for both. We may be sure that the Boer will not trouble us, unless we first trouble him.

From the same paper, which always speaks of the brave men who are fighting for their freedom as " cowardly, murdering Boers," I take the following account of the Boer leaders :—" The president of the discontented farmers is a man of about sixty years of age, a native of the district of Cradock, Cape Colony, and is one of the ' voertrekkers ' or original emigrants from the Old Colony, who trekked north to the Vaal river, while another branch came over the Drakensburg to this colony. Those ' trekking ' northwards remained longer isolated than the others ; and several travellers have noticed the almost Chinese or Japanese jealousy with which they kept strangers out of the country. The Krugers settled in the fertile district behind the Magaliesberg range ; and the subject of our notice became a leader amongh is people, known as the ' Doppers '—a kind of extremely strict body of Dutch Protestants ; in fact, a peculiar people in dress, manners, and mode of life. ' Oom Paul,' as he is affectionately called, came first into prominent notice at the time of the civil war (as it was called) between the northern Boers and those of Utrecht, Wakkerstroom, and Lydenderg—who had a kind of commonwealth of their own. Paul commanded the northmen, and after an engagement, in which one man was actually killed and Nikolas Smith was wounded, they fraternised ; and the Republic started anew under Pretorius, son of the Pretorius who was head of the Boers of Natal after the death of Maritz and Retief. Personally, Mr. Kruger is of middle height. He is much respected by all who know him as an honest man and sincere patriot. During the troubles which ended in the annexation of the Transvaal, Mr. Kruger fearlessly helped his country's cause in purse and person. He has made two journeys to London, protesting against the Annexation ; and although he has seen and appreciated the power of Great Britain, he has not hesitated to throw his lot in with the insurgents."

P. J. Joubert, the Commander-in-Chief of the Boer armies, is one of those who reached the country *via* Natal —the family leaving this colony on its conquest, or, rather, acquisition, by the British Government. Yet the subject of

our notice did not go far, as his "woonplaats" almost joins
the Colony at its northernmost point; and he has many
relations living in our midst. In many ways Mr. Joubert
is a remarkable man, and may be called self-educated, until
manhood never having seen any book but the Bible and
Psalter. Indeed, he informed the writer of this notice that
he was 19 years of age before he saw a newspaper. Mr.
Joubert has also led some expeditions against Kaffirs in the
early days of the Republic, and some of his detractors say
he was very severe on the natives in these raids. He was
Vice-President during the rule of President Burgers, and
acted as President during His Honour's absence in Europe,
when the misconduct of Mr. Cooper at Lydenburg is said
to have produced the Sekukuni troubles, which stopped the
flotation of the National Loan through Itsinger and Co.,
of Amsterdam, and caused the final financial collapse of the
Republic. He also has been accused of being unduly in-
fluenced by a certain legal luminary, late canteen-keeper in
Natal, now Advocate in the Supreme Court of the Transvaal. But no one has ever impugned his honesty of purpose
or patriotism. Mr. Joubert was Kruger's colleague in the
mission to London on both occasions. He is younger than
" Oom Paul," and the improvement in his gait, dress, and
manner on his return from London was remarkable. Mr.
Joubert had adopted Bond Street fashions even to the
attenuated umbrella—rather a change from the home-made
turn-out of the veldt farmer under ordinary circumstances.
One of the anomalies of this gentleman's political ideas is,
that he swears to have the independence of the Transvaal;
but, as a compromise, he would vote for Sir Theophilus
Shepstone to be President of the Republic. During his
short visit to this city to see Sir Bartle Frere, Mr. Joubert
freely expressed his opinions, saying openly that he regretted the step this people were driven to, as it was certain
to retard the progress of the country and the people for
many years. The compromise he would accept to-morrow
is this—Governors to exercise authority in the name of the
Queen, but to be elective as were the Presidents. Restoration of the Volksraad, with additional town members com-

mensurate with their rise. Treaty of offence and defence with South African Colonies. Compact or project of law, for repayment of Imperial advances, *sine quâ non*. No patronage to be exercised by any authority or person foreign to the land.

Dr. E. F. Jorissen is the legal adviser of the leaders of the people, or, as they call it, "Staats Procureur;" a doctor of divinity, and was a clergyman of some celebrity in Holland, and is known to entertain very broad and liberal views on ecclesiastical matters. He was brought from Holland by President Burgers, was inspector of education under that gentleman's government, and at the change which took place in 1875, was made Staats Procureur or Attorney-General. Dr. Jorissen is an extremely learned and talented man; but he has been too long a clergyman, with the privilege of having all the talk to himself, to subside at fifty years into a cool debater, and his temper is somewhat of the shortest. He is an irreconcilable, especially since his personal views were ignored, and his office treated with very scant courtesy at the time of the Annexation.

Edouard Bok, the "Secretaris," is the youngest of the quartette, is a native of Holland, although his family reside at present in Brussels. He is a good specimen of an educated foreigner. His command of the English language and acquaintance with its literature is extensive. He accompanied the deputation as interpreter and scribe. He is about thirty years of age; he is a studious, thoughtful, and withal, gay, genial man, who will probably make his mark in the world.

I now leave the case in the reader's hands. We have sinned through ignorance, and all that I seek is that justice and truth may triumph over prejudice and interest and passion.

CHAPTER II.

THE TRANSVAAL AND THE BOERS.

It is vain to dispute the fact that those Puritan Fathers—who, upon one occasion, held a meeting, and resolved first that the earth was the Lord's, and the fulness thereof; secondly, that it was the heritage of the saints; and that thirdly, they were the saints, and were, therefore, justified in depriving the natives of their grounds, and in taking possession of them themselves—had a full share of that English faculty of appropriation which has made England the mistress of the seas, and for awhile, almost, the ruler of the world; and, as Englishmen, we cannot say that on the whole that wholesale system, which has planted the British flag in every quarter of the globe, has been disastrous to the communities ruled over, or dishonourable to the nation itself. In some cases undoubtedly we have acted unjustly; in some cases the lives and happiness of millions have been placed in incompetent hands; in some cases we have had selfish rulers and incapable officers; but India and Canada and the West Indian Islands and Australia and New Zealand are the better for our rule. An Englishman may well be proud of what his countrymen have done, and it becomes us to review the past in no narrow, carping, and censorious spirit. We have spent money by millions; but then we are rich, and the expenditure has not been an unproductive one. We have sacrificed valuable lives, but the men who have fallen have been embalmed in the nation's memory, and the story of their heroism will mould the character and fire the ambition and arouse the sympathies of our children's children, as they did those of our fathers in days gone by; and yet there is a danger lest we undertake responsibilities beyond our means, and find ourselves engaged in contests utterly needless in the circumstances of the case, and certain to result in a vain effusion of blood and expenditure of money. As far as South Africa is concerned, this is emphatically the case. Originally the Cape Settlement was but a fort for the protection of Dutch ships on their way to India. When we took it from the Dutch, it was but a small colony at the best, and now one Colonial Governor tells us we must annex the whole country as far as the Zambesi. This is rather an expensive operation, and it is not pleasant to the British taxpayer to be told, as was stated by Mr. Noble, an official of Natal, at the meeting of the Colonial Institute a year or two since, that if we are true to the position and privileges which Providence has assigned us in giving us such rich possessions on the threshold of Africa, we have before us the glorious destiny of working towards the regeneration of a whole quarter of the globe, of extending the domain of freedom and the boundaries of Christian civilisation into the interior of the Dark Continent. Of course, the sentiment was received with cheers. The Colonials were present in great force on the occasion, and the more money we spend on South Africa the better for them ; but the sentiment is one very natural to the British nation, which appears to believe that the universe was created for the sale of Manchester cottons, Birmingham muskets, and Sheffield ware ; and it is also one very dear to Exeter Hall, which is always asking, in accents more or less emphatic but feminine—

" Shall we to lands benighted
The lamp of life deny ? "

forgetting how ready is the retort, " Physician, heal thyself," and the contrast there is between the modern missionary and the Apostles, who, in accordance with the Divine command, went forth to preach the Gospel. Few Englishmen will deny that it is a blessing greatly to be desired that men should become Christians, whether they be black or white, and equally ready are they to admit that commerce is the surest bond of peace and creator of national prosperity.

But a question may be raised as to how Christianity is to
be best spread, and as to how the true interests of commerce are to be advanced. Sir Bartle Frere, the recent
ruler of South Africa, may be considered to be the head of
the school of which Mr. Noble is an illustrious exponent.
To another of that school, Sir Theophilus Shepstone, we
owe the annexation of the Transvaal. Sir Arthur Cunynghame, late Lieutenant-Governor and Commander of the
Forces in South Africa, is of a similar way of thinking.
Already he begins to talk of future annexation. The Orange
Free State, he tells us, must join the South African Confederation. We must have a harbour in Delagoa Bay,
which the award of Marshal Macmahon, unfortunately for
the true interests of that part of the world, handed over to
the Portuguese; and we must have a further slice of Zululand. Thus it appears, while Sir Bartle Frere plunged us
into a bloody contest in Zululand, in which we gained
no glory, and which already has tarnished the honour of our
flag; now that is over, the process of annexation in the
interests of commerce and Christian civilisation will still
have to go on. Before, in such a cause, the British soldier
has shed his last drop of blood, and the British taxpayer
has parted with his last farthing, it is well to pause, and to
ask what are the results of Imperialism in South Africa,
and whether the investment is remunerative. Of course,
money can do everything. As I once heard an old farmer
say, you can grow turnips on the top of your head if you
only put enough soil there; but, then, that is a question of
cost, and the general impression is—right or wrong, I stay
not here to inquire—that such a mode of raising a turnip
crop is anything but economical. With money we can crush
out all the savage hordes, not of Cetewayo alone, but of all
the Kaffirs whom we have allowed to increase and multiply
in our midst. With money we can plant missionaries in
every fever-stricken swamp, all over the African continent.
At present the number and diversity of missionaries is
somewhat a perplexity to the inquiring Zulu, but that perplexity will vanish as he sees how these Christians love one
another; and if he be inclined to underrate them, and to

treat them disrespectfully, in time he will know better. Captain Aylward writes that a missionary, himself, and another were on their way from Bushmans to Mooi River, when a Zulu passed by the missionary, and saluted him as "Umbunga." " My companion was instantly off his horse, and, being a powerful, active man, nearly six feet six inches high, made no difficulty in catching the nigger, whom he held easily with his left hand. He said a few words in Kaffir, and then set vigorously to work thrashing his captive, who, grovelling on his knees, yelled out incessantly, ' Inkosi! Umfundisi! Umfundisi! Inkosi!' When the flogging was over, I asked my clerical friend what was the matter, and what was the meaning of the scene. He said, with much delight, evidently thinking he had done a most virtuous action, ' The black villain saluted me as " Umbunga " (white man), although he could plainly see by my dress I was an Inkosi and a teacher. I have, however, taught him to respect my robes.' " If all our missionaries are thus muscular, and thus ready to redress a wrong, real or imagined, it is evident we may expect results which may be received with cheers in Exeter Hall. Conversion will proceed apace.

To understand our rule in South Africa, we must first realise our exact position there. The colonies, taken altogether, are about 450,000 square miles, or equal in size to united Germany, France, Belgium, and Holland. The total population is rather more than two millions, of which about 440,000 persons are white. With the exception of Delagoa Bay, there is not a good harbour all along the coast. The country is subject to drought, and seems chiefly to be inhabited by diamond diggers, ostrich farmers, and wool growers. Its great agricultural resources are undeveloped, because labour is dear, and all carriage to the coast is expensive. The English never stop in the colonies, but return to England as soon as they have made a fortune. Living is quite as dear as in England, and in many parts dearer. In the Cape Colony the chief amusements of all classes are riding, driving, shooting, and billiards. In the interior there are fine views to be seen, and in some quarters an abundance of game. The thunderstorms are frightful; the rivers, dry in summer, are torrents in winter. The droughts, the snakes, the red soil dust, and the Kaffirs, are a perpetual nuisance to all decent people. "Although South Africa is a rising colony," writes Sir Arthur Cunynghame, " I hardly think it offers to the emigrant the chances which he would obtain in Australia or New Zealand. South Africa is not a very rich country. Labour is hard to obtain, and it will be years before irrigation can be carried on a sufficient scale to make agriculture a brilliant success. Nevertheless, land is so abundant that the energetic colonist is sure, at least, to make a living, and provided he does not drink, has a good chance of becoming a rich man." A great deal of money is made by ostrich farming and sheep grazing, but they are occupations which require capital. As to cereals, it pays better to buy them than to grow them. A cabbage appears to be a costly luxury, and the price of butter is almost prohibitive. " South Africa," wrote a *Saturday Reviewer* recently, " is the paradise of hunters, and the purgatory of colonists." The remark is not exactly true, but for all practical purposes it may be accepted as the truth. If this be so, how is it, then, it may be asked, we English have been so anxious to get possession of the country ? The answer is, We hold the Cape of Good Hope to be desirable as a port of call and harbour of refuge on our way to India; but the opening of the Suez Canal has changed all that, and the reason for which we took it from the Dutch in 1806 does not exist now. Whether the country has ever made a penny by the Cape remains to be proved.

In taking possession of the Cape of Good Hope, we found there a people whom we have annexed against their will, and of whom we have made bitter enemies. These were the original Dutch settlers, or Boers, mixed with whom were descendants of the French Huguenots—a primitive, pastoral people, with a good deal of the piety of the Pilgrim Fathers, and who set to work to exterminate the pagans much after the fashion of the Jews, of whom we read in the Old Testament. Their plan of getting rid of the native

difficulty was a very effective one. They either made
the native a slave, or they drove him away. Mr.
Thomas Pringle, one of our earliest colonists, says,
"Their demeanour towards us, whom they might be supposed naturally to regard with exceeding jealousy, if not
dislike, was more friendly and obliging than could, under all
the circumstances, have been expected." They were, he
says, uncultivated, but not disagreeable, neighbours, exceedingly shrewd at bargain making; but they were civil
and good-natured, and, according to the custom of the
country, extremely hospitable; and the same testimony has
been borne to them by later travellers. They lived as
farmers, and the life agreed with them. The men are finely
made, and out of them a grand empire might be raised. In
1815 they made an effort to shake off the British yoke. A
Hottentot, named Booy, appeared at the magistrate's office
at Cradock, and complained of the oppressive conduct of a
Boer of the name of Frederick Bezuidenhout. Inquiry
was accordingly made. The Boer admitted the facts, but,
instead of yielding to the magistrate's order, he boldly
declared that he considered this interference between himself and his Hottentot to be a presumptuous innovation
upon his rights, and an intolerable usurpation of authority.
He told the field-cornet that he set at defiance both himself
and the magistrate who had sent him on this officious
errand, and, to give further emphasis to his words, he fell
violently upon poor Booy, gave him a severe beating, and
then bade him go and tell the civil authorities that he
would treat them in the same manner if they should dare
to come upon his grounds to claim the property of a
Hottentot. It must be remembered that when the Boers
were handed over to us, without their leave or without their
consent being in any way asked, each Boer had perfect
control over the liberty and life and limb of every Hottentot
under his control. It was only thus he believed his property
was safe, and his throat uncut. But to return to Bezuidenhout. The Cape Government could not allow his defiance
to pass unheeded. An expedition was sent out against him,
and he was shot. The affair excited a great sensation in

the country. At a numerous assemblage of the Boers in
the neighbourhood it was resolved to revenge his death.
They did more; they resolved to be independent of the
hateful British yoke; but, it is needless to add, in vain.
England, after putting down Napoleon, and triumphing at
Waterloo, was in no mood to be defied by a handful of
Dutch farmers in a distant quarter of the globe. But the
Cape Government had Kaffir wars to fight, and they could
not afford to treat the Boers as absolute enemies, and they
were rewarded with a large portion of the territory won
from the Kaffirs in 1819. But this was not sufficient for
their earth-hunger. They crossed the boundaries, and, with
their lives in their hands, planted themselves among the
savages. In 1838 they went off still further from British
rule. In that year the slaves were manumitted, and a sum
of money was voted as a compensation to the Boers. To
the shame of the British Government, it must be confessed
that the equivalent was never paid them. Despairing of
ever receiving it, they sold their rights to Jews and middle-
men, and trekked far out into the country into the districts
known as Griqualand, Natal, the Orange Free State, and
the Transvaal. It is because we have followed them there,
when there was no need to have done so, that we are now
engaged in a costly and bloody war. First we seized Natal,
then we took possession of the Diamond Fields, and our
last act was the annexation of the Transvaal. How far
this system of annexation is to spread it is impossible to
say. It is equally impossible to state what will be its cost
in treasure and in men. It seems equally difficult to say
upon whom the blame of this annexation system rests. It
really seems as if we were villains, as Shakespeare says, by
necessity, and fools by a divine thrusting on. We should
have left the Boers alone. They were not British subjects,
and did not want to be such. Natal was not British
territory when they settled there, neither was the Orange
Free State Territory; and, at any rate, in 1854 their
independence, which had been persistently fought for, and
nobly won, was acknowledged by the British Government
as regards the Orange Free State and the Transvaal.

Surely in South Africa there was room for the Englishman and the Boer, and if it had not been for the dream of Imperialism, which seems to dominate the brain of our colonial rulers, the two nations might have lived and flourished side by side. The Boer, at any rate, has made himself at home on the soil. It agrees with him physically. In the Orange State and the Transvaal he made good roads, and built churches and schools and gaols, and turned the wilderness into a fruitful field. In reply to the English who pleaded for annexation, he said, " We fled from you years ago ; leave us in peace. We shall pay our debts early enough ; your presence can but tend to increase them, and to drive us through fresh wanderings, through new years of bloodshed and misery, to seek homes whither you will no longer follow us. We conquered and peopled Natal ; you reaped the fruits of that conquest. What have you done for that colony ? Do you seek to do with our Transvaal as you have done with it—to make our land a place of abomination, defiled with female slavery, reeking with paganism, and likely, as Natal is, only too soon to be red with blood?" But when this was our English rulers had made up their minds to get rid of the innumerable complications of South Africa by a Confederation—of which no one is mad enough to dream now.

" The Transvaal," wrote one who knew South Africa well —the late Mr. Thomas Baines—" will yet command the admiration of the world for the perseverance, the primitive manliness and hardihood of its pioneers." As a proof of advancing prosperity, when he was there in 1860 its one-pound notes had risen in value till four were taken for a sovereign, and several hundred pounds' worth had been called in and publicly burnt upon the market-place. It is a proof of the simplicity of the people that on that occasion the Boers and Doppers (adult Baptists) crowded wrathfully around, and bitterly commented on the wastefulness of their Government in wickedly destroying so much of the money of their Republic ; while others, of more advanced views, discussed the means of raising them still further in value, and sagely remarked that because they had been printed in Holland the English would not take them, but that if others were printed in London they would certainly be as good as a Bank of England note. In the Volksraad (House of Commons) now and then some amusing scenes occurred. The progressive party wanted, one day, to pass some measure for the opening and improvement of the country, when the opponents, finding themselves in a minority, thought to put the drag on by bringing forward an old law that all members should be attired in black cloth suits and white neckerchiefs. This had the immediate effect of disqualifying so many that the business of the House could not be legally conducted; but an English member who lived next door, slipped out, donned his Sunday best, with a collar and tie worthy of a Christy Minstrel, and resumed his sitting with an army that completely dismayed the anti-progressionists. Sir Arthur Cunynghame testifies to this simplicity as still the characteristic of the Dutch. "Some little time before our arrival," he writes, "a German conjurer had visited this distant little village, when the Doppers were so alarmed at his tricks that they left the room in which he was exhibiting, and, assembling in prayer, entreated to be relieved of the devil who had come amongst them." Sir Arthur adds the story of a Jew, who in dealing with a Boer had made a miscalculation, which the Boer pointed out, appealing to his ready-reckoner. Not in the least taken aback, the Israelite replied, "Oh, this a ready-reckoner of last year!" and the poor Boer was done. A further illustration of their simplicity is to be found in the fact that when they trekked from the Cape they fancied that they were on their way to Egypt, and, having reached in the Transvaal a considerable river which falls into the Limpopo, thought they were there, and called it the Nyl—a name which it still retains. In accordance with their serious teaching, they gave Scriptural names to their settlements and villages; and if they were severe on the natives, and ruled them with a rod of iron, did not the Jews act in a similar manner to the Hivites and Hittites, and did not Samuel command Saul to hew Agag in pieces before the Lord?

Major Ashe, the latest writer on the subject, in his history of the Zulu campaign, thus ably describes the African Boers:—" The typical Boer is doubtless a pattern of hospitality, simplicity of heart, fondness for his home and family, and of those general domestic attributes which are so dear to an Englishman. But in his relations and contact with the native races and real owners of the soil, the Dutch Boer seems to lose all sense of reason and justice, and to remember only those early and blood-stained annals of pioneering, when the white man and the black neither gave nor asked for quarter in their struggle for supremacy in the land. Indeed his intolerance of a native is so intense that he cannot be induced to look upon him as a human being, but he regards the unfortunate aboriginal as a wild beast to be hunted and shot down. But the Boer has his fairer side, although his type has as yet been un-changeable. As he existed when he ruled in Cape Colony in 1808, so he now exists in the present day in his settle-ments in the interior. He is uneducated, uncultivated, unprogressive, and obstinate ; but he developes qualities under adverse circumstances which must command English respect. He is certainly domestic as far as his own family circle, but, at the same time, the reverse of gregarious in regard to the world in general. When he first commences to farm and settle he likes to possess not less than 6,000 and not more than 20,000 acres of good undulating ' veldt.' When he has obtained this, he starts in his waggon with his wife, his children, his scanty supply of goods and chattels, his cattle and sheep, and his only literature, the family Bible. He selects a good spring of water, being careful that no neighbour is located within at least ten miles. He builds his house with one large central hall, with the kitchen in rear, and four or five bedrooms opening out of the hall, all on the ground floor, and sometimes with a wide verandah outside. Kraals for his cattle, fences to his garden, and enclosures of 50 or 100 acres are quickly run up ; and so fertile is the soil and so favourable the climate, that in four or five years his garden will be full of oranges, lemons, citrons, peaches, apricots, figs, apples, pears, and vines. His herds and flocks multiply, his wheat and Indian corn thrive, and thus he lives in a rude but grateful abundance. His sons arrive at manhood and marry; his daughters are sought as wives, and if the land is good and plenty they remain and farm near, and for each generation and new family a new house is built a few hundred, yards from the original. More acres with each generation are brought under the plough, and the man who is a good farmer, good father, and good husband cannot be brought to see that he must not covet his neighbour's land when that neighbour happens to be a black man! Without sentiment, without tenderness, and without a particle of enthusiasm, and with the most circumscribed intellectual horizon, he has a stubborn practicability which is admirably suited for the work of a pioneer, but which never developes into a power of civilisation amongst savage tribes."

It is to be feared that the Boers have never had justice done to them by our rulers. We had no claim on them. It was to escape British rule that they, with their wives and children, their men-servants and maid-servants, their oxen, and their sheep, their horses and their asses, went forth into the wilderness. Even Mr. Trollope admits that when they took possession of Natal, " there was hardly a native to be seen, the country having been desolated by the King of the Zulus. It was the very place for the Dutch, fertile without interference, and with space for every one." There they would have settled, as did the Pilgrim Fathers on the other side of the Atlantic, and built up a flourishing State, but we followed them, and drove them away. If they had been allowed to remain, the English Government and the English people would have been saved a good deal of trouble. At any rate, we should never have heard of the native difficulty in Natal—the difficulty which keeps away the emigration required to develop the resources of a country happily situated in many respects; the difficulty which must ever be felt by a handful of English in the presence of a horde of polygamous and untutored savages who will not work, and who, alas! are not ashamed to beg. Natal, had

the Dutch been left peaceably in possession of it, would
have been by this time the home of a God-fearing, civilised
community, instead of swarming with Pagans who have fled
there from the cruelties of their native kings, and who learn
to treat their protectors with insolent contempt. In Natal,
the English shopkeeper has to speak to his customers in
their own language. Where the Boers hold sway it is
otherwise. In the Dutch parts of the Cape Colony, Captain
Aylward writes: " The coloured people are tame, submissive, and industrious, speaking the language of their in-
structors and natural masters. As I proceeded further on
my journey through the Transvaal," continues the same
writer, " I saw in various directions gardens, fruitful
orchards, and small, square houses in the possession of
blacks, who were living in a condition of ordinary propriety,
having abandoned polygamy and other horrid customs
resulting from it. So great an improvement I had not
noticed during any part of my previous residence in Natal."
It is a pity that we have made the Boers our enemies ; and
the worst of it is, in their determination not to be English
the women, according to Captain Aylward, have been a
wonderful aid to the men. They have suffered for that
spirit. It has called them from the homesteads built by
their fathers, the rich lands where the grapes clustered
and the sheep fattened, and the fields were white for
the harvest. In 1841 Major Charteris wrote : " The
spirit of dislike to English rule was remarkably domi-
nant among the women. Many of those who had formerly
lived in affluence but were now in comparative want, and
subject to all the inconveniences accompanying the insecure
state in which they were existing, having lost, moreover,
their husbands and brothers by the savage, still rejected with
scorn the idea of returning to the colony. If any of the
men began to drop or lose courage they urged them on to
fresh exertions, and kept alive the spirit of resistance within
them." Sir Arthur Cunynghame has nothing but praise for
the Boers. On his way to the Diamond Fields he stopped at
Hanover, which, he says, " has a grand appearance, the
Dutch minister's house, standing in the centre, being quite

a palace." It was built by the subscriptions of his parishioners. The honours which the Dutch lavish on the ministry are worthy of remark. Equally worthy of remark is their hospitality and their piety. The farmer gives his guest the best entertainment he can provide, and "before the family retires to rest the large Bible is opened and the chapter appropriate to the day is read." On another occasion, Sir Arthur's party encamp near the residence of a rich Dutch farmer, who refused admission to his house, and would not even sell them an egg; yet he records the fact that, "late in the evening the sounds of the Evening Hymn floated over the plain, the nasal twang of the patriarch being distinctly heard leading the choir, while female voices, with their plaintive notes, chimed in. It is pleasant," adds Sir Arthur, " to hear in these lone lands such evidence of a religious sentiment pervading the community, and it is an assurance that the people are contented and happy." Sir Arthur writes :—" There are no finer young men in the world than the young Dutch Boers, who are generally of immense height and size, and very hardy. Their life is spent in the open air by day, and frequently at night they sleep on the veldt, with no tent or covering. Men more fit for the Grenadier Guards, as to personal appearance, could not be found. Some of them are plucky. A Boer had part of his hand blown off by the bursting of his gun. Having no doctor near, he directed his son to bring his hammer and chisel, and shape off his fingers." As an Irishman, Captain Aylward is enthusiastic as regards the personal charms of the ladies. Many of the elder ones even, he admits, are not uncomely, and in the wild neighbourhood of Lydenberg itself, he tells us, are to be seen some bearing traces of beauty of no ordinary character, whose lives, he says, somewhat unnecessarily, are useful, adorning, and cheering the homes of their husbands and children. These people are somewhat unlettered, and very phlegmatic. "They do not wish," writes Sir Arthur Cunynghame, " to move ten miles from their own door, nor to see one who comes from ten miles beyond it." Their moral discipline also seems somewhat severe. " In the little fort," writes Captain Aylward,

" was an English storekeeper, named Glynn, whose daughters had a piano, on which they would occasionally play dance and other profane music. This was a source of great annoyance to their pious neighbours, who, in many respects, resembled our early Puritans. It was requested that the piano should be silenced, as the music might tempt the anger of Heaven if persisted in during a time of war and trial. If a girl in the laager were frivolous or light in her conduct, she was liable to be arrested, and brought for trial before the Fathers of the Church, from whom she might receive a severe caution, or even the punishment of removal." At Lydenberg, at the time of Sir Arthur's visit, an altercation had taken place on the unrighteousness of dancing, for which a party was tried by the Synod; but an appeal was made to the Court, and this appeal formed an important epoch in the history of the town. To show how primitive these Boers are, let us take the following story :— A schoolmaster was lately appointed in Zoutspanberg. One of his earliest lessons was to teach the children that the world turned upon its own axis. He also endeavoured to make them understand the revolutions of the heavenly bodies. The children went home, and were impertinent to their parents, and told them that the earth went round the sun. The elders of the district met, and consulted regarding these new doctrines, and finally agreed to refer the subject to the minister, who requested the schoolmaster to explain. The schoolmaster said, "I teach them nothing but the movements of the heavenly bodies, and that the earth revolves round the sun." The minister answered, " Well, this may be true, no doubt, and what the earth does in Holland ; but it would be more convenient at present if, in the Zoutspanberg, you would allow the sun still to go round the earth for a few years longer. We do not like sudden changes in such matters." The schoolmaster took the hint, and the sun continued to go round the earth as usual. The power of the minister of a parish is very great. A great deal depends upon him for the improvement and well-being of the town. Many a time it was said to Sir Arthur, when he observed that a town was flourishing,

" Yes, we are fortunate in our minister ; " and when it was
falling back·it was, " Ah ! all will alter when we get rid of
our present minister."

I call one witness more—Lieut.-Col. Butler, who, in his
"Rovings Re-told," tells us :—" The Boer is a fearless and
practised rider and an unerring shot. Life in the ' Veldt'
is familiar to him in all its aspects. He can rough it with
any man, tame or wild, the world over ; nevertheless he is
not a soldier ; he will fight Zulu or Bechuana or Basuto,
but then he will have the long flint ' roeer' against the
arrow or the assagai, or the Westley-Richards breech-
loading rifle against a rusty musket. He is ever ready
to take the field : his rifle and gun are in the room-corner ;
his ammunition-pouch is ever full ; his horse (knee-haltered
or in the stable) he can turn out at short notice. Nevertheless he is not a soldier, and he never will be one. In one
of the many boundary disputes arising out of the diamond
discovery, a party of Boers and Englishmen met in opposition near a place called Hebron, on the Vaal River. As is
frequently the custom in such cases, the anxiety for battle
diminished with the distance between the opposing forces,
and a parley was proposed by the respective leaders when
the hosts came within shooting proximity. There hap-
pened to be in the ranks of the party a native of Ireland,
who naturally did not at all relish the pacific turn affairs
seemed to be assuming. While the leaders debated the
settlement of the dispute, Pat left the ranks of his party,
and, approaching the place of consultation, demanded of
his chief (now busily engaged with the Boer commandant
in smoking and debate) if he and his friends on the hill
might be permitted to open fire upon their opponents
before any further discussion on the cause of quarrel was
proceeded with. The Boer, alarmed at this sudden pro-
position to defer diplomacy to war, asked the meaning of
such a bloodthirsty request. ' The boys want the word to
fire,' replied Pat, ' because they are so mortal hungry.'
Not altogether perceiving the force of the reasoning, but
deeming it wise to remove such an evident *casus belli*, the
Boer commander at once sent forward a sheep and an ox

to appease both the food-hunger and thirst for blood o
the opposite side; and as the map of South Africa presents
Hebron on the Vaal River without those two crossed swords
indicative of a field of fight, it may be presumed that
matters ended with no greater sacrifice of life than that
of the animals which Pat led back in triumph to his
hungry comrades."

It is to the credit of these people that they have a consistent native policy. No faith is to be held with Rome.
"Delenda est Carthago" is their motto. They leave the
natives to quarrel among themselves, while our English
policy has been to play off one petty savage chief against
another, and to arm and strengthen the natives with whom
we are ultimately to fight. The natives see through this,
and argue, as Sir Arthur Cunynghame testifies, that the
English fear them, else why, they ask, do they give them such
high wages? or why do the Government allow them to buy
arms? It is some such feeling that urged on Cetywayo into
his unfortunately hostile attitude. He considered that we
were his allies against the Boers, and thought we annexed
the Transvaal for him and his savage followers. Up to the
annexation he and the English were on friendly terms. At
the commencement of the Zulu war, it seemed that the
Boers were reluctant to fight for English rule, and some of
the colonial papers hinted that they were a danger and a
menace. Was that to be wondered at when we remember
how we have always sacrificed them to the natives? The
Free States newspaper complained that "our British
neighbours have established at the Diamond Fields free
trade in guns and ammunition, in spite of all treaties with
the Republic, and even in spite of their own professed
policy in the Cape Colony. Griqualand West permits the
supply of guns and ammunition to the natives—Zulus and
Basutos—without hindrance, whilst Earl Carnarvon requests
all South Africa to meet in a friendly conference, because of
the native question and Zulu difficulty. British traders
supply Her Majesty's enemies and ours with guns and
ammunition to any extent, in order that they may be
better prepared to fight us when the next struggle may

commence; and, worst of all, British commerce, represented by colonial shopkeepers and merchants, who, to fill
their own pockets, would not for a moment hesitate to
bring ruin on the colonial farmers and Republican Boers,
cry out that it is preposterous to stop the trade in guns."
Assuredly, the Boers had ample reason to complain of the
Imperial policy in South Africa. There is little to be said for
our dealings with them after they had removed out of our
rule. That we had no right to annex the Diamond Fields,
the sum we offered in compensation may be considered as
fair evidence; and the annexation of the Transvaal, besides
being a crime, was a blunder for which we are now paying
dearly in person and in purse. It has been shown that the
cry for annexation raised was merely " an ignorant expres-
sion of the dissatisfaction of a mean and contemptible
minority "—a set of greedy speculators and disreputable
office-seekers, who grossly deceived the English officials,
who were not naturally averse to the power and prestige a
new command would give them. The Republic was not
insolvent, nor was it unable to hold its own. In the war
with the Basutos, contrary to the assertion of Mr. Trollope,
the Burghers were everywhere victorious, nor was it stained
with slavery, as, if so, when Sir Theophilus Shepstone
immediately annexed it, we should have heard of a wholesale emancipation; nor was the step taken by the will of
the people. The only argument for the step was that we
were obliged to take it in order to prevent our own house
catching fire, and the result has been the conflagration
we were so anxious to avoid. Sir Theophilus Shepstone
annexed the Transvaal, and our house caught fire in
Griqualand West, and Secocoeni broke out war into war;
and, lastly, we had the tragedy of Isandula. We shall
never be safe till we have the Transvaal, argued Sir Theophilus Shepstone and his friends. Then, argued the latter,
now that we have the Transvaal, we are bound to go to
war. This reasoning was irresistible to Lord Chelmsford,
who, in a despatch dated September, 1879, says, " So long
as Natal and the Transvaal had separate interests, the
policy of the chief of the Zulu nation was to play off the

former against the latter. . . . With the annexation
of the Transvaal this state of things virtually came to an
end.''

Well, we annexed the Transvaal, and scarcely a word was
said about it in the House of Commons. However, when
the General Election was impending, and a gigantic effort
was to be made to place the Liberals in office, great statesmen were not backward in protesting against what they had
sanctioned in Parliament. Mr. Gladstone, as was to be
expected, was especially emphatic. He who has pleaded so
powerfully the cause of the Bulgarian Christians, who con-
tended against such cynical scoffers as Mr. Lowe, that the
unenfranchised to whom he was about to give votes, were
our own flesh and blood, naturally had something to say
for the Boers. In his Midlothian speeches in 1878-9 this is
what he did say :—

'' The Government have annexed in Africa the Transvaal
territory, inhabited by a free European, Christian, Republican community, which they have thought proper to bring
within the limits of a monarchy, although out of 8,000
persons in that Republic qualified to vote upon the subject,
we are told, and I have never seen the statement officially
contradicted, that 6,500 protested against it. These are
the circumstances under which we undertake to transform
republicans into subjects of a monarchy.''—*November 25th*,
1879.

'' The Transvaal is a country where we have chosen, most
unwisely, I am tempted to say insanely, to place ourselves
in the strange predicament of the free subjects of a monarchy going to coerce the free subjects of a republic, and to
compel them to accept a citizenship which they decline and
refuse. But if that is to be done it must be done by force.''
—*November 26th*, 1879.

''You have the invasion of a free people in the Transvaal.''
—*December 5th*, 1879.

'' We have undertaken to govern despotically two bodies
of human beings who were never under our despotic power
before, and one of them who were in the enjoyment of
freedom before. We have gone into the Transvaal territory,

where it appears—the statement has not been contradicted—
that there were 8,000 persons in a condition of self-govern-
ment, under a Republican form. Lord Carnarvon announced,
as Secretary of State, that he was desirous of annexing their
own territory if they were willing. They replied by signing
to the number of 6,500 out of 8,000 a protest against the
assumption of sovereignty over them. We have what you
call 'annexed' that territory. I need not tell you there
are and can be no free institutions in such a country as that.
The utmost, I suppose, that could be done was to name
three or four or half a dozen persons to assist the Governor.
But how are they chosen? I apprehend not out of the
6,500, but they are chosen out of the small minority who
were not opposed to being annexed. Is it not wonderful to
those who are freemen, and whose fathers had been freemen,
and who hope that their children will be freemen, and who
consider that freedom is an essential condition of civil life,
and that without it you can have nothing great and nothing
noble in political society, that we are led by an Administration, and led, I admit, by Parliament, to find ourselves in
this position that we are to march upon another body of
freemen, and against their will to subject them to despotic
government."—*Birthday Speech, 29th December*, 1879.

" The Prime Minister spoke of his difficulties in Europe
and difficulties in Asia. He omitted, gentlemen, Africa ; he
did not say we had created any difficulties for him there ;
but there he has contrived, without, so far as I am able to
judge, the smallest necessity or excuse, to spend five millions
of your money in invading a people who had done him no
wrong ; and now he is obliged to spend more of your money
in establishing the supremacy of the Queen over a community, Protestant in religion, Hollanders in origin, vigorous
and obstinate and tenacious in character even as we are
ourselves, namely, the Dutchmen of the Transvaal."—
March 18th, 1880.

Unfortunately, the Boers have taken Mr. Gladstone at
his word. It is a pity they forget how circumstances alter
cases—how, out of office, a statesman talks in one strain,
and in office another.

But to return to South African Imperialism. *Ex uno disce omnes.* One example will suffice of the way in which that theory of dominion universal, from the Cape to the Zambesi, which appears to dominate over the official Englishman, when he has anything to do with Africa, acts in a mischievous manner, may be seen in the case of Griqualand East, formerly called No Man's Land, which was some years since a sort of neutral territory. In time the Griquas, or bastards, settled there. They were an industrious people, and far more advanced in civilisation than any other native tribe. They had large flocks of cattle and sheep, and were wealthy, with good furniture and houses, and prospered under the rule of their President, Adam Kok. Many new buildings, such as churches and schools, were being erected when Sir Cunynghame visited them, and many new stores put up. He writes : " In the afternoon we attended the native service carried on in the Dutch language. It was impossible for me to follow it ; in fact, the discovery that the sermon related to the Prodigal Son formed the limit of my knowledge of what was going on. The congregation appeared attentive, and the clergyman in earnest." Not long after the visit, it was decided by the British that they should annex the country, and Adam Kok was pensioned off with a thousand a year, which he did not, however, long enjoy, as he was soon killed by a carriage accident. At a meeting of the people on the subject, Captain Adam Kok complained, as, indeed, he had every reason to do, of the hasty and arbitrary manner in which Government were assuming authority in his country. They had their own cannon, fire-arms, and ammunition, bought with their own money, and after being left for thirteen years entirely to their own resources, without any preliminary notice, he said, the Cape Government stepped coolly in and took possession of them and their property. When the Government laid out the Kat River Settlement of Hottentots, they gave the settlers seed, corn, ploughs, and various other things to help them. But the Griquas were not so treated. They had to do everything for themselves, and we were bound to regard them not as enemies to be put down, but as friendly allies to be encouraged and preserved.

How long is this system to be pursued? The Transvaal, I wrote in 1879, is getting into a worse state every day. It has vast resources which cannot be developed. It is importing flour, when it might be a great corn-producing country. It has no manufactures, and its exports are few. Captain Aylward writes:—"The Boer party complain bitterly of the annexation. They say our liberties have been unnecessarily taken from us, and our country annexed, not only against the will of the majority, but in utter defiance of Lord Carnarvon's instructions, which state that no such proclamation shall be issued by you (Sir Theophilus Shepstone), unless you shall be certain that the inhabitants, or a sufficient number of them, or the Legislature, desire to become our subjects." The Boers also object to the annexation, because they believe that the arguments put forward by Sir Theophilus Shepstone are not borne out by facts, and they are still more angry because they believe the annexation was brought about by false pretences, accompanied and strengthened by attacks made upon their honour and character by a party Press interested in their destruction. They say further, that the terms of the Annexation Proclamation have not been adhered to, and this party, undoubtedly the strongest in the country, appeals to England to do them justice and restore to them their country. The railway party who want a connection with the natural outlet of the Transvaal, Delagoa Bay, are discontented, and so are the very men who were the first to applaud annexation. As it is, it seems, the Transvaal must end either in anarchy or martial law, and will be a heavy burden on the British tax-payer for many years to come. Mr. Trollope himself admits that it is not easy to justify what we have done in the Transvaal. "If there be," he writes, "any laws of right and wrong, by which nations should govern themselves in their dealings with other nations, it is hard to find the law in conformity with which that act was done." And Mr. Trollope is right. Undoubtedly it was an act of injustice of which we have not yet seen the bitter end. There is little chance of that injustice being undone. The Dutch are poor and far away. It is the old, old story of the wolf and the lamb over again. We have made so little of South Africa, we might leave the Boers alone. All that we can say against them is that when it was the fashion for West Indian planters to maltreat their slaves, they often did the same.

The Boers (this was written in 1879) are becoming more discontented, as well they may, and there is no sign of this discontent ceasing. In the beginning of February, 1879, they held a large meeting at Wonderfontein to receive the report of the visit of the deputation, Messrs. Kruger and Joubert, to Europe. The latter is reported to have said :—
" My brethren and fellow-countrymen,—I am very glad to see you all spared by God in this our beloved country. I wish and hope the best, also, with regard to your families. You have deputed us on a mission of the utmost importance to yourselves. I know you are awaiting our report with deep anxiety. I know your feelings and your wishes—aye, I share your anxiety, and, therefore, *I* will not detain you long by words. Know, then, that I cannot report to you so favourably as you had expected that the all-powerful British Empire had acknowledged your rights so that you may, as had been said by Joshua to Caleb, be strong and possess the country which God has given you. No, brethren, England has annexed your country, and will keep it, and I may not mislead you by telling you that you cannot stop the superior power of England. Therefore, take heed for yourselves, and don't do anything of which you may repent for ever, and which may plunge yourselves, your families, and others into deeper misery still. Pray to God for wisdom ; be prudent, and act wisely. Who knows, God may help us and grant relief. You had sent us to ask back your independence. What we have done for it you already know from the newspapers, and the rest you will learn from the books or pamphlets which we had printed. In how far you will decide that we have done our duty we leave to you. I do not care for myself, but I do for the country, and the people, and where I feel my own shortcomings and weak-

ness, I am satisfied before God and my conscience that I, if *I* have not obtained what you, what I, and the people have desired, I have done for it what I could. And with this I wish God's greatest blessings for yourselves and the country." Other speeches were delivered of a more angry and exciting character. It was intimated that we got our Empire by robbery. Mr. W. Pretorious said the High Commissioner promised much, but all he wanted was to get back his independence. Said another speaker, amidst enthusiastic cheers, England might annex and oppress them, but it could never give them an English heart. Some resolutions were moved, of which the following was one :—
" The committee, supported by the people, cannot be satisfied with the reply of the English Minister, Sir Michael Hicks-Beach, and resolve to continue to protest against the injustice committed, and, further, to devise ways and means with the people for attaining their object." After the meeting, some people having torn to pieces the printed copies of Sir Bartle Frere's letter, Mr. Joubert strongly condemned the stupid proceedings, and requested the people to act wisely and with judgment. On the Sunday religious services were held, and on Monday a further meeting took place. Ultimately it was resolved, " That the committee, having learned the opinion of the people expressed in their memorials, and the expressed wish of the people not to submit to British supremacy, but to abide by the protest of April 11, 1877, proposes to the committee a deputation to acquaint Sir Bartle Frere therewith, and at the same time to assure His Excellency of their full co-operation for the advancement of the whole of South Africa, provided the annexation be rescinded." Clearly, I wrote in 1879, when we have settled with Cetewayo, we shall have a little trouble with the free people of the Transvaal. According to the *Natal Mercury* of that date, we had better leave them alone.

The following, says the *Natal Witness*, is a translation of the oath of mutual allegiance taken by a great number of respectable Transvaal Boers at the Wonderfontein meeting. It will strike most people that this oath is the oath of men who are to be respected. It will also strike them that such men are likely to secure the sympathy of the great bulk of the English nation :—" In the presence of Almighty God, the Searcher of hearts, and praying for His gracious assistance and mercy, we, burghers of the South African Republic, have solemnly agreed, for us and for our children, to unite in a holy covenant, which we confirm with a solemn oath. It is now forty years ago since our fathers left the Cape Colony to become a free and independent people. These forty years were forty years of sorrow and suffering. We have founded Natal, the Orange Free State, and the South African Republic, and three times has the English Government trampled on our liberty. And our flag, baptized with the blood and tears of our fathers, has been pulled down. As by a thief in the night has our free Republic been stolen from us. We cannot suffer this and we may not. It is the will of God that the unity of our fathers and the love to our children should oblige us to deliver unto our children, unblemished, the heritage of our fathers. It is for this reason that we here unite, and give each other the hand as men and brethren, solemnly promising to be faithful to our country and people, and looking unto God, to work together unto death for the restoration of the liberty of our Republic. So truly help us, God Almighty."

Till Sir Bartle Frere appeared upon the scene at the Cape, men ridiculed the idea of another Kaffir war. Then all was changed. The following is an extract from a letter, dated February 12, 1879, received by a gentleman in London from a well-known merchant at the Cape :—" Who is responsible for the fearful loss of life which has taken place in Zululand? This is now the question of all questions; but we fear that it will drop out of sight, as the iniquitous proceedings perpetrated here during the late so-called war have done. The Zulus will, of course, be crushed, as ' Might is Right' seems now to be England's motto. Sir Bartle Frere and Lord Chelmsford must answer for the part they have played, and for the consequences of the tragedy they have caused. Never was there a greater mistake than the Frere-Sprigg native policy. We have not right on our side, and we have not the force to carry it out, even if we had. We have made enemies of the loyal Gaikas, of the Basutos, of the Fingoes, of the Zulus, and of every other tribe in South Africa, by our harsh and unjust treatment of them. The appointment of Sir Bartle Frere as Governor, and of Mr. Sprigg and his party to power, are the greatest misfortunes which have befallen this country for fifty years."

The South African correspondent of the *Daily News*, writing from Maritzburg, March 2, 1879, says :—" It is now only too evident to every one that Sir Bartle Frere's policy has been most mischievous in its effects upon South African interests. More has been done since he landed at Capetown, two years ago, to produce discord and· unsettlement than, it is to be feared, can be undone for many years to come. Friendly tribes have been exasperated; colonists have been ridden over rough-shod, and now it would seem that the High Commissioner is bent on bringing about the last and final evil, by engaging in a war of conquest with the Transvaal Boers. There is a strong and increasing feel-ing throughout South Africa that the annexation of the Transvaal must be reversed. When that act took place it met with very wide approval, for two reasons—first because it was believed that the majority of the Boers were consenting parties ; and next, because it was believed that the act might tend to bring the two great European nationalities closer together. The return of the second Transvaal deputation has brought to light the fact that the majority of the Boers were by no means consenting parties. They complain, too, and justly, that not one of the promises made at the time of the annexation had been fulfilled. If the acts of the annexation were repealed, and time allowed for the bitter feelings engendered by it to subside, there is little doubt that the Boers would be found willing to come into some sort of confederation with the other South African States, and there can be no doubt that if the Transvaal came in willingly the Free State, whose capital, Bloemfontein, is regarded by many as the natural capital of South Africa, would come in also."

What is to be the end of our system of annexation in South Africa? Our Pro-Consuls far away from the healthy criticism of the English Press, and possibly better trained in ancient than modern history, dream imperial dreams, and the public at home applauds when a magnificent success crowns their work. In the case of Sir Bartle Frere there has been a failure, and he will have to pay the penalty; while demagogues who, like the Irishman who when landed in America, and asked for his vote for the opposition candidate, immediately promised it, remarking he was "again all Government," see in the failure the hand of Earl Beaconsfield, and hold him up to scorn and contempt. It is clear what has been done at the Cape is only in accordance with the whole past of colonial rule, not merely there, but in every quarter of the globe. We could not leave the Boers alone, who stood as buffers between us and the surrounding savages. We must follow them over desert and plain and swamp and river and rock and bush. The colonist reaped, at any rate, a benefit from such a policy, for he made profitable contracts for his waggons and horses, and there was a refreshing stream of English gold, which otherwise would have been dried up. The Book of Nature might say, Leave the Boers and the savages alone; but to a highly-cultured people the Book of Nature is a blank, and the passions and prejudices, and fears and hopes, of the passing hour are the only considerations by which the public and the puppets it places in office are moved. Some of us still talk of the New Testament; but he who were to quote it, even after Mr. Speaker had said his prayers, in our High Court of Parliament, as bearing in any way on national policy, would be as much laughed at as Dr. Kenealy or Major O'Gorman. Meanwhile time will solve the problem—the storm will blow over. The mob and the pictorial papers will glorify the returning heroes who have crushed a savage who was mad enough to defy on his own behalf and on that of his people the British power, and the British public will have to pay the bill—not, unfortunately, the hard-working, over-taxed working man; he is a myth, as much so as a mermaid or a griffin; but that large middle-class, on whom the tax-gatherer instinctively preys; who have been shorn so often that it has become to them a second nature; who have been the mainstay of the country, but who are fast becoming, under the weight of Imperial taxation for Imperial schemes, an extinct race.

CHAPTER III.

OUR KAFFIR WARS.

WRITING two or three years ago, Captain Aylward, in his work on the Transvaal, indicated that South Africa would be a burning question for the British taxpayer in the summer of 1879. That period of time has passed, but before then the question came to the aggrieved individual aforesaid in an unpleasantly novel and alarming manner. In spite of instructions from home, Sir Bartle Frere at once initiated an aggressive war on the Zulu nation, which represented an expenditure of a million and a half, and which, before it was fought out to the bitter end, occasioned the expenditure of a much larger sum. In a time of unexampled commercial distress, when thousands of homes have been made desolate ; when tender and delicate women who have been nursed in luxury and comfort have been deprived of their daily bread ; when grey-haired old men have found themselves after the struggle of a life made paupers ; when the most the majority of us can do is to meet the inevitable expenditure of the passing day—we were committed, in accordance with the Imperial instincts of officials in high quarters, to a warlike policy of which none could tell the result or calculate the cost. This, alas! is no new thing where our South African colonies are concerned. A war is begun by a blundering ruler, or in accordance with the wishes of interested parties, and the ignorant public at home has to pay the bill. Sir Arthur Cunynghame, in his last work, expresses the hope that for the Kaffir wars which were in existence when he was at the Cape the British taxpayer would not have to pay ; nevertheless, in the Budget

£344,000 are put down for the Transkei War. Mr. Trollope goes a step further, and plainly shows that the colonist, whether as farmer or labourer or trader, is much better off than men of the same class at home, and that it is unjust we should be taxed by an immense military expenditure for their benefit alone. Speaking of the Transvaal, he adds, "Great as is the Parliamentary strength of the present Ministry, Parliament would hardly endure the idea of paying permanently for the stability and security of a Dutch population out of the British pocket." But Parliament will take money out of British pockets with which to fight the Dutch population. It is to be questioned whether we as a people have been pecuniarily benefited by South African colonies. They offer no such advantages as a field of emigation as New Zealand or Canada or Australia. The emigrant is afraid of a Kaffir War, and he goes elsewhere. If the colonists had to pay for their own wars, we should have had fewer of them, and by this time they would have been in a much more flourishing condition. Nor should we have been trembling, as we were at one time, lest any morning we might hear the Zulu army had marched into Natal and had not left a white man alive to tell the tale of the terrible tragedy that ensued. I maintain there will be no end to these Kaffir scares and Kaffir wars so long as the men and money of the mother country are so employed, and so long as the colonial governors are allowed to rush into war. If a man goes to live in South Africa he should do so with the feeling that he runs a certain risk, and that knowledge would make him live on good terms with the natives. High interest, as the late Duke of Wellington is reported to have said, means bad security. In a similar manner, we may say, cheap land means bad security; and the farmer who buys the freehold of his farm in Natal for less than the rent he has to pay for it at home cannot expect to be as secure in purse or person as a farmer in the Weald of Kent.

War is the inevitable result of the way we have gone to work in South Africa. In the sparsely-peopled land of North America the key-note of settlement is struck at the moderate figure of 200 acres to the settler ; in South Africa it has been fixed at twenty times that sum ; and 4,000 acres make the minimum of land upon which the pioneer of civilisation will begin his work. And what is the result ? Why, that in South Africa our settlers spread themselves farther and farther out in defenceless isolation—people a territory as large as France with the population of a tenth-rate English town—drive the natives back into more compact masses outside our frontiers, who, naturally covetous of the lands of which we have dispossessed them, are anxious and ready to fight with us whenever an opportunity occurs. Very clearly we are shown that the late Zulu war was the result of the annexation of the Transvaal. "For thirty years," writes Colonel Butler, "the emigrating Dutch had acted as a buffer between us and the native races. By the annexation of the Transvaal we removed that buffer and placed ourselves face to face with the black man along seven hundred miles of frontier. Nay, we did more than that, we stepped at once into a legacy of contention, oppression, and injustice, from which it was almost impossible to escape." In the Diamond Fields we created a new danger, inasmuch as it brought together all the representatives of the various black races scattered over the continent; bands of twenty tribes whose common brotherhood has been laid ages and ages ago, amidst the wars and wanderings of a time before the white man came. In the vast school-room at Kimberley, the prizes given were rifles and ammunition; the lesson taught was identity of interest against a common foe.

Lieutenant-Colonel Butler may well complain that in these busy times people have no time to inquire into an injustice, and that they quickly grow tired of the whole subject. And even the novelty of an unrighteous war soon wears off. Still we cannot but quote what he has to say on the origin of native wars:—"There is nothing more easy, said a veteran Cape statesman to the writer, than to get up a war in South Africa. If I had only known that the Government wanted such things, I could have given them a score of Kaffir wars in my time. He spoke the soberest truth. A wild or semi-wild man is always ready to fight if wrong be put upon him. It is the only method of obtaining redress or vengeance that he knows of. He has no means of separating the acts of irresponsible white men from the government under which they live. The only government he can understand is that personal rule which makes the chief and the subject alike answerable ; and hence every trader carries with him, in his dealings with natives, the character of the nation to which he belongs. Yet wherever I have gone, among wild or semi-wild men. I have found one idea prevalent in the minds of white men trading with natives. That idea was that it was perfectly fair and legitimate to cheat the wild man in every possible way. One hundred years ago it was considered right to cheat the black man out of his liberty and sell him as a slave. To-day it is the natural habit of thought to cheat the black man out of his land or out of his cattle. In the coast region of Natal the coin known as a florin is called among natives a Scotch half-crown. The reason of the title is simple. A few years ago an enterprising North Briton went to trade with the natives in that part of the country. He did not barter— he paid cash for what he bought. Curiously enough he always tendered half-crowns in payment. Months later the natives found that their half-crowns were worth only two shillings each ; and since that time the florin, along the coast, bears the name of ' Scotchman.' Instances of a similar kind could be multiplied until the reader would be tired of their iteration."

What is to be done with the African is a question which concerns us all. America, at the time of its discovery, said to contain fourteen million Indians, to-day does not contain four hundred thousand. Alas ! for us, the African will not die off like the Indian. Nor can we much wonder that we do not find him a hopeful subject from the missionary point of view. " In nine cases out of ten," writes Lieutenant-Colonel Butler, " we have taken or bought or tricked his land from him ; we have killed or chased away the wild animals that roamed upon it ; we have shouldered him out into the remote mountains or regions unfitted for our present wants. He learns our knowledge after a little time ; but that is only as a light held out to show how miserable is the position he has accepted—the position of a Christian pariah." In one respect, certainly, the Boers were wiser than ourselves. In our greed for diamonds we gave the natives all the guns and ammunition they required. It was our diamond diggers who gave the Zulu king the power, to crush which, we had to enter on a war for which the British taxpayer had somewhat heavily to pay ; while the greedy colonist pocketed his golden gains. South Africa altogether is an expensive luxury. The colonists will not work. All that we get is wool, ostrich feathers, diamonds. Farming is quite at a discount, and yet there the land is specially fitted for the farmer and the agriculturist. The only farmer was the old-fashioned Boer, at one time hospitable and ever ready to welcome the stranger at his gate ; now naturally a hater, and with good reason, of the British name.

In 1811 was our first Kaffir war. It was waged on our part in the most cruel manner—no quarter was given by the white man—no prisoners taken—all were slaughtered till the Kaffirs were driven backwards and eastwards across the Great Fish River. In 1819 we had another fight, as was to be expected. Wars lead to wars. What the sword wins the sword only can retain. Lord Charles Somerset, who had Imperial ideas of the most pronounced character, took it into his head to elect Gaika as the sole head of Kaffirland, when in reality the paramount chief was Hintza. In 1818, by seizing the wife of one of the latter's chief councillors, and other aggressive acts, Gaika drew upon himself the enmity of his superior, and was defeated in a fierce battle with great slaughter. After the defeat Gaika appealed to the British Government to assist him, not in bringing about a reconciliation, but in making war on his enemies. Accordingly a powerful force of regular troops and armed colonists, to the number of 3,352 men, under Cólonel Brereton, was despatched to fight on behalf of this wretched savage. The reward of their valour consisted in more than 30,000 head of cattle, of which 21,000 of the finest were given to the colonists and the rest to Gaika. As a natural consequence, the plundered tribes, rendered desperate by famine, crossed the Fish River in great numbers, drove in the small military posts, and compelled the border colonists to abandon their dwellings. Additional troops were sent to the frontier, and a plan was formed for the re-invasion of Kaffirland. But before that plan was carried out, the Kaffirs, to the number of 9,000, led by Makanna, attacked Grahamstown, and would have taken it had not the leader, in accordance with the custom of the heroes of his country, sent a message overnight to inform Colonel Willshire, the British commandant, that he would breakfast with him next morning. This gave the British time to prepare, and the result was 1,400 Kaffirs were left dead on the field. After this Colonel Willshire and Landdrost Stockenstrom advanced into the enemy's country, carrying fire and slaughter everywhere. At length Makanna, to obtain better terms for his people, freely surrendered himself into the hands of the English; but this act had no effect on the latter, who proceeded to drive away the Kaffirs and to annex 3,000 square miles of fertile territory. The Kaffir, of course, became more incensed against us than ever. He saw his lands taken away, and an inferior chief placed, as it were, in power; but for a while, however, we had no regular fighting, only occasional brushes in consequence of cattle stealing, real or pretended. There is a foray recorded in the *Cape Government Gazette* of 1823 as a very meritorious affair. At daybreak on the 5th, Major Somerset, having collected his force, passed with celerity along a ridge, and at daylight had the satisfaction of pouring into the centre of Makanna's kraal with a rapidity that at once astonished and completely overset the Kaffirs. A few assegais were thrown, but the attack was made with such vigour that little resistance could be made. *As many Kaffirs having been destroyed as it was thought would evince our superiority and power*, Major Somerset stopped the slaughter, and secured the cattle to the amount of about 7,000 head.

Strange to say, this mode of impressing the Kaffir with the fact of our superiority and power only made matters worse, and the commissioners of inquiry had to report, in July, 1825, that the annexation had entailed expenses upon the Government and sacrifices upon the people in no degree compensated with the acquirement of the territory which was the object of it. A similar remark may be made at the present time, for, as soon as a colony gets strong enough, its first effort is to fight the mother country with a hostile tariff. It seems then, as now, nothing was easier than to get up a *casus belli*. Mr. Thomas Baines, the great African traveller, illustrates in an amusing manner what is meant by justice to the natives by some of our colonists. "I was speaking to a friend," he writes, "respecting the new discoveries, and we both agreed that it would be wrong to make war upon the natives and take the gold-fields away from them." "But," said my friend, "I would work with foresight. I would send cattle farmers to graze their herds near the borders, and the Kaffirs would be sure to steal them; but if not, the owner could come away, and he could even withdraw his herdsmen and let them run night and day, then the Kaffirs could not resist the temptation. We could go in and claim the stolen cattle, and if the Kaffirs resisted and made war, of course, they would lose their country."

Our next Kaffir war was, as all our Kaffir wars were, discreditable to ourselves. The war was not only, writes Mr. Trollope, bloody, but ruinous to thousands. The cattle were, of course, destroyed, so that no one was enriched. Of the ill-blood then engendered the effects still remain. Three hundred thousand pounds were spent by the British. But at last the Kaffirs were supposed to have been conquered, and Sir Benjamin D'Urban triumphant. Lord Glenelg himself, however, declared that the Kaffirs had "ample justification." It seems to an impartial observer that the war was entirely brought about by the English. After his expulsion from the Kat River, Macomo, the son of Gaika, retired to the banks of the Chumie, but so far from instigating his people to plunder the colony, he appears to have done his best to restrain them. On that head we have abundant testimony, but it suited the Colonial Governor to have him and his brother Syalie removed, and removed they were under really aggravating circumstances.

Our own soldiers did their work well, and we have graphic pictures of burning villages, ruined cultivations, and people driven away like wild beasts. The chief was sulky, writes Colonel Wade, and well he might be. Another cause of the war was the frontier system, which constantly led to collisions with the natives. As the Chief Tyalie declared, " Every year a commando comes, every week a patrol comes, every day farmers come and seize our cattle." It was then the infuriated natives swept over the colony, to be in turn driven back. The murder of the great chief Hintza appears to have been an extraordinarily brutal one. " It is stated to me," writes Lord Glenelg, " that Hintza repeatedly cried for mercy, that the Hottentots present granted the boon, and abstained from killing him ; that this office was then undertaken by Mr. Southey, and that then the dead body of the fallen chief was basely and inhumanly mutilated."

Under Sir Peregrine Maitland we had a fourth Kaffir war. Almost his first act was to commit an unpardonable sin in Kaffir eyes—the erection of a fort in their territory. As they said in their own expressive language, the new chief smelt of war, and war soon came. A Kaffir stole an axe ; he was sent to Grahamstown to be tried at the circuit court. The chief Tola said that was contrary to the treaty that all such offences were to be tried at Fort Beaufort. The plea was in vain—the man was sent ; an attempt was made to rescue him, and a Hottentot policeman was shot. At once the English took the field to avenge the insult in blood.

In 1850 the fifth Kaffir war arose, and the inhabitants of one advanced military village after another were murdered. This went on for nearly two years, but was at last suppressed by dint of hard fighting. It cost Great Britain, wrote Mr. Trollope, upwards of two millions of money, with the lives of about four hundred fighting men.

Our Natal territory cost us a little war initiated by Sir George Napier in 1841. At first the war went very much in favour of the Dutch. Then a larger force came, and the Dutch succumbed to numbers. It was not, however, till

1843 that the twenty-four still existing members of the Volksraad declared Her Majesty's Government to be supreme. In the case of the Orange Free State we had a war which resulted in our beating the Dutch and winning the place, only to relinquish it again. Our rule in Natal led to our little war with King Langalibalele, who had come to live in Natal as king of the Hlubi tribe, who is now living, after a good many lives had been lost, near Cape-town at an expense to the Government of £500 a year. In England it was felt that the chief had been unfairly used, the trial was adjudged to have been conducted with over-strained rigour, and the punishment to have been too severe. There would have been no war at all had it not been for the blunders of mischievous go-betweens. Then came the Zulu War, of the bitter incidents of which it is needless to speak. And now once more we are at war, and a cry has been raised for the extermination of the Boers as an independent nation ; and when that is over, there will be fresh hordes of hostile natives to be fought, new lands to be annexed, a scientific frontier to be gained, and the colonists will make fortunes out of the millions thus spent. I ask in sorrow, How long is England to be strained and denuded of men and money for these costly wars ? Surely it is a reproach alike to the Christianity and Statesmanship of our time that we have not yet hit on a more excellent way.

CHAPTER IV.

A PLEA FOR THE KAFFIR.

At the present moment—this was written in 1879—we are witnessing a sorry spectacle for a Christian nation : that of a whole people hemmed in in one corner of Eastern Africa, waiting to be swept off the face of the earth by the finest soldiers and the most scientific instruments of murder England has at her command. Their crime has been that in defending their native soil from the tread of the foe, they annihilated an English regiment, and for such an act there is no hope of pardon, in this world at least. From every corner of the land, from the pulpit and the Press, from the hut of the peasant and the palace of the prince, from the cad of the music-hall and the statesmen of Downing Street, there has risen a cry for revenge; and that we shall take a full and fierce revenge there can be no doubt. Already in England and in Africa the blood-stained demon of war has sown her seed and reaps her harvest; already there have been bitter tears shed over hundreds of fallen heroes in desolated homes, and women wail and children vainly cry for loved ones whose bones now bleach the distant plain of Isandula. And there will be sadder and darker tragedies yet to come if the wild instincts of the people are to be gratified and the Zulu Kaffirs are to be exterminated. They are now represented as savage hordes, whose existence is incompatible with English rule. Let me plead that they are not such as they are represented, and that it is better that we make them friends. Cetawayo, by not crossing the Tugela and sweeping with fire and slaughter through Natal when that colony lay stricken and terrified at his feet, has set us an example of forbearance which it were wise to imit.te. If we fail to do so, the blood feud between us and his people can know no end. They in their turn will nurse a spirit of revenge, and the Kaffir wars of the future will be fiercer and more cruel than any we have hitherto known.

There is much in the Kaffirs that should make them friendly with the English people if fairly treated. One well-known writer states that they are keen observers of character, and have great contempt for a man who gets drunk, or who does not keep his word. Kaffirs should be treated with kindness, fairness, and firmness. They have an accurate idea of justice, and appreciate the administration of just legislation, wrote Mr. Wilson, late a resident magistrate in Natal. In their wild state they are innocent, quiet, unoffending, and hospitable, and it is only when they live close to a European town that they acquire the bad habits of the white race, and with the cunning instincts natural to them become dangerous to the community. Said another colonist, at a conference recently held at the African section of the Society of Arts, mentally they were equal to white men. Dr. Mann, who has lived twenty-five years in Natal, and who has written a large work on that colony, declares that the Kaffirs had great ability, and, even without education, seemed a much higher race intellectually than the lower class of the agricultural population in England. In fact, he would rather go to a Kaffir for a response to an appeal to his reason than to an English labourer. Twenty years ago said Mr. Richardes, they brought comparatively nothing, but now they were great customers to the British merchant. As a further proof of how a Zulu Kaffir could rise in the world, Dr. Mann mentions the case of one he knew who could not read, who borrowed on his own credit £500 to buy a sugar mill, and obtained a further loan from the Government to get it to work, and who, in three years, paid off the loan, and became a prosperous manufacturer. It seems a pity to kill off such people—a people by nature intended to be our customers and allies and friends. Much more than this may be said. "Kaffirs seem," writes Lady Barker, " a very gay and cheerful people, to judge by the laughter and jests I hear from the groups returning to their kraals every

day by the road just outside our fence." A similar testimony
was borne by Mr. Robert Richardson in a paper read by
him a year or two since at a meeting of the Society of Arts.
" The Zulu," he said, " may not be dignified, but manliness
and good temper are written on his cheerful countenance ;
and he is not only groom and cattle herd, but domestic
servant, and performs with alacrity the least honourable
service about a house. If Natal lambs don't skip, as the
Surveyor-General once said, at least the Natal servant does,
for his errands are done at a trot, cutting capers, while he
sings with an appearance of great enjoyment in his own
music. Brimful of humour, he is essentially a laughing
animal, and having few wants or comforts, he rivals Mark
Tapley in being jolly under creditable circumstances. All
things considered, the Natal Zulu is a better servant than
the (Cape) frontier Kaffir."

There is much that is good in these Kaffirs. A correspondent of the *Cape Mercury* wrote : " It is said the Kaffir
language has no word for gratitude ; but, nevertheless, the
Kaffirs are not all void of it. A native man in good circumstances lent a brick waggon gratis to convey Mr. Conway
and family to the house of his father-in-law, Mr. Conway
being at the time very ill. Unfortunately, after his arrival,
he died, leaving his wife and family not very well off. The
other day the native arrived to take home his waggon which
he had kindly lent, and found that if he took it he would
leave Mrs. Conway without any means to make an independent living. To the astonishment of all present, he
said, ' I don't forget good deeds done to me by Conway
before poverty overhauled him, and to show that I am
sincerely sorry for his family I here make you, his widow,
a present of my waggon and gear now in your possession to
enable you to provide for his children.' The value of the
waggon was £60."

In contrast with this is the utter indifference displayed by
too many colonists as to the welfare of the Kaffirs. " The
other day," says a writer in a Colonial paper called the
Independent, " a wheelbarrow tumbled over the Kimberley
(Diamond fields) reef on to the head of a Kaffir. His master,

with some irritation, inquired of the employer of the careless servant, ' Do you want to kill my Kaffirs ? ' The reply was an indignant query, ' What about my wheelbarrow? It's smashed, and your Kaffir isn't hurt.' "

But enough of this. According to all writers the Kaffir is deeply impressed with a sense of English superiority. Let us now show him our true superiority ; that we war not with him, that we desire not his land, that we are as merciful as we are strong. Cetewayo's young men have washed their spears in blood, and ours have fallen under circumstances which have created an abiding sense of their heroism in every Zulu breast. Have we no wise men among us who can stand between the living and the dead, and calm the natural passions of the hour, and stay the ravages of war ? If there be not such, our task is an endless one to fight and conquer, merely to fight and conquer again. The soldier cannot solve the difficulty ; he merely postpones it for a time.

Failing to do justice to the Kaffirs we are left to a very undesirable alternative. If we cease to rule by kindness, we must do so by brute force. Contemplating this delightful state of things, the *Natal Witness* of the 8th of February says :—" Civilisation has become unmistakably aggressive. The result which it was hoped might be gained by the quiet influence of the plough-share and the railway, is now destined to be effected, under the guidance of Sir Bartle Frere, at the point of the bayonet. The great herald of peace, whose feet were to be so beautiful upon the mountains, has become the genius of war. Whether Sir Bartle Frere foresaw this, we are not aware, nor are we aware whether he likes his position. We will not even argue whether he is right or wrong in believing that civilisation must be aggressive. Judging by history, we incline to the opinion that he is right, and if he is right, then the hope of producing the social amalgamation we have referred to was a vain hope altogether. But whether it is a vain hope or not, let us not deceive ourselves about one thing—that it is now extinguished. The ship of State has been put about on the other tack, and is at the present moment, it must be

owned, making very bad weather of it. Whatever is now
done by way of civilising the native population in South
Africa must be done by force. We do not necessarily mean
such physical force as is employed in a pitched battle. We
mean rather this—that the native population must hence-
forth be ruled by a show of military strength rather than by
trust in British justice or regard for commercial advantages.
This, we say, may be right ; it may in the very nature of
things have been unavoidable. But do not let us deceive
ourselves about it. The fact is so, and we must make the
best of it or the worst. If the Home Government will be
content to keep a large military force in South Africa for
thirty years to come, and if South Africa can afford to pay
for it ; or if, failing this, the British taxpayer will be kind
enough to pay for the protection of the colonies which will
not be worth protecting if he does not pay—if all this comes
to pass, then for thirty years South Africa will be a place
which, though utterly useless as a field for immigration, a
place in which certain classes of people can live. But then
will these things be done? Will England be content to
keep such a body of troops in South Africa? Can South
Africa pay for them? And, if South Africa cannot, will the
British public pay? These are questions most seriously
affecting our future, and which for the present we leave to
be answered by our readers as best they may be able."
Such is a colonial aspect of what is emphatically a colonial
question.

We hear in these days so much about the Zulu that we
are apt to forget that in South Africa we have any one else
to deal with. In fact the coloured people with whom our
whites more or less come into contact, are estimated by
Mr. Trollope, our best authority on the subject, at 3,000,000,
and with the exception of the Korannas, and the Bushmen,
who inhabit Namaqualand, a region where only copper is to
be found, are a very superior race of men, well-built, with
good capabilities, mental and physical. It is to be questioned
whether the danger in the recent system of government at
the Cape, which places power in the hands of the white
colonists alone, is not calculated to create discontent among

the numerous and high-spirited people around. It is much to be regretted also, that we have not yet been able to adopt a steady and consistent policy with the native tribes. The great civilising agency of our time is the British trader, and at the Kimberley mines he has set the native to work; but more than this is required if the native is to be elevated and to be taught to take his proper place as a labourer in the great harvests of the world.

If the reader looks at a map of South Africa, he will find that it is divided into many districts, some of them of immense extent—hundreds of miles apart, and inhabited by peoples under varying rulers, and with varying interests. The Cape, for instance, has little sympathy with Natal, and the great Namaqualand has little in common with the Transvaal. In the latter country, as is well known, we have a community hostile to English rule, while the Orange Free State, on each side hemmed in by English dominions, maintains a precarious independency of its own. A grand South African confederation is a beautiful idea; but there does not seem much chance of carrying it out just now. Meanwhile we go on annexing all the surrounding country, much to the discontent of the natives themselves.

At present the great difficulty is the native population. According to all accounts, they are in an unsettled and agitated state. Of the original Hottentot we do not hear much. Mr. Trollope believes that the bulk of the population of the Western Province of the Cape Colony is Hottentot, who has, however, long given up all idea of independence. The Dutchmen and the Englishmen also, who are to be met with in the East and West alike, are not likely to give much trouble; but as we get further from the Cape, and the white population is sparser, the difficulties increase. It is true there is no chance of a Kaffir scare in that part of Africa bordering on the Atlantic, nor in the Kalakari desert on the North is there any danger to be apprehended; but it is as we get nearer the Indian Ocean, and especially after we have crossed the Kei, and come into Kaffraria proper, that we find ourselves in the presence of a native population, always required to be watched with a careful eye. There dwell the Galekas, who, to the number of 66,000, under Kreli, have only recently been put down. They and the Tembus, and the Pondos, and the Bomvanas, and the Fingos, inhabit all the district till Natal is reached. Amongst some of them a British Resident resides; in all they do pretty much as they like. Of Natal and its 300,000 Kaffirs it is needless to say more here. In the same neighbourhood are the Griquas; but they are bastard races. The Balongas of Thaba 'Ncho, who dwell under the shelter of the Orange Free State, and the Basutos, are a branch of the Bechuanas, who inhabit that part of the Kalakari desert bordering on Griqualand and the Transvaal. Of the black African races, the South-Eastern people whom we call Kaffirs and Zulus are, probably, the best. They are not constitutionally cruel; they learn to work readily, and they save property; but even at the Cape, where they will have power at the voting-booth, Mr. Bowker, the late commandant of the Frontier Mounted Police, says:—"As a nation, they hate the white man, and look forward to the day when he will be expelled the country." Mr. Trollope remarks of the native that he is a good-humoured fellow, whether by nature a hostile Kaffir, or submissive Fingo, or friendly Basuto; but, if occasion should arise, he would probably be a rebel. The two names most familiar to the English readers are the Gaikas and Galekas, who have both given us a good deal of trouble. Sandilli, with his Gaikas, have long been subjected, though they have not been regarded as peaceable as the Fingos and the Basutos. The total population of the region beyond the Kei is stated to be 500,100, of whom, with the small exception of the Griquas, all are Kaffirs.

Our special friends among the natives are the Fingos—a tribe originally driven from Natal by the warrior Chaka, among the Galekas, by whom they were enslaved and regarded as Kaffir dogs. We English took pity on them, released them from slavery, and settled them somewhere near the coast between the great Fish River and the Keishamma, and their old masters, the Galekas. There they were a perpetual eyesore to their former masters. In the first place, they had for their 50,000 souls 2,000 square miles, while that left for the 66,000 Galekas was not more than 1,600 miles. Again, the Fingos have been a money-making people, possessing oxen and waggons, and gradually rising in the world. For a time, as was to be expected, mischief between the two tribes was brewing, and in 1877 a drunken row precipitated the two into war. We rushed into the war to defend the Fingos, and Kreli, who had no desire for a struggle with the English, was beaten, and his country annexed. The Basutos, who have given up fighting since the days of their great king Moshesh, number about 127,000. In the map they are now included in the Cape Province; but they border the Orange Free State— lying between it and Kaffraria. In 1868 they became, after a wearisome contest with the Dutch, so worried by the latter, that they implored the British to take them as subjects. The Basutos are not Kaffirs, but a branch of the Bechuanas, as are the Balongas, who live peacefully under the shelter of the Dutch in the Orange Free State. As their land is the very best on the Continent for agricultural purposes, they have bought a great many ploughs, are great growers of corn and wool, and naturally, as is the case with such people, are friends of peace and great lovers of money. At one time they were cannibals. For a long time they were terrible fighters, and that they have become what they are may be quoted as a fine testimony to the civilising influences of the trader. At the same time, it will not be difficult to make enemies of them. One of their chiefs— Morosi—has, taking advantage of the Zulu war, attempted a little *emeute* on his own hook. We are glad to find, as was to be expected, that he has got the worst of it. In a letter dated March I, from Alrival North, the writer says :—" I wonder the Government are not more active in their movements, and send a proper force to crush him at once, as it is believed here that if Morosi gets the least advantage the whole of Basutoland will be in a blaze. Sprigg will find that the Disarming Act will cost the colony more than he expected, and the Basutos, who are supposed to be loyal, are not at all inclined to give up their arms, and

I am sure will not do so without a struggle." Sir Garnet Wolsley said as much, and the prophecy has been fulfilled. We are now at war with the Basutos, and the following is their petition which has been addressed to England :—" The petition of the Basuto chiefs for peace is signed by Lerothodi, Letsea, Joel Molappe, and other chiefs of Basutoland, and is sent to Sir George Strahan on behalf of themselves and their people. They state that for 12 years they have lived peacefully under the Queen's Government as loyal subjects paying all taxes, and using arms in defence of the interests of her Majesty. They refer to a petition from Letsea, their late paramount chief, to Sir Bartle Frere, making the same declaration of loyalty. They complain that the Cape Government was confiscating their land for the benefit of Europeans, which was believed to be the beginning of the confiscation of the whole of Basutoland and the extermination of the rightful owners. Next came the order to disarm, although the only arms they had were purchased under permits from Government officers, and had been used, and were ready again to be used, in defence of the Queen's sovereignty. Mr. Sprigg (the Cape Prime Minister) himself said that the Basutos should not be disarmed ' until the surrounding tribes had been disarmed and a strong protective force established in Basutoland. This protective force has never been established, though promised. The Basuto people will willingly and cheerfully obey the laws and orders of her Majesty the Queen, but we pray you to beseech her Majesty to allow us to retain our arms and our country. We pray you also to beseech her Majesty to cause war and bloodshed to be stopped in our country. Our fields are being devastated, our homes destroyed, our wives and children have to flee to the mountains for shelter, where many perish of hunger and disease. Her Majesty too is a woman. We know we are unable to fight the white man. We do not want war. We want peace. Give us peace. We have always been told that her Majesty is powerful, but just also. Therefore we believe she will hear this our prayer.' "

The latest phase of the Basuto question (says the *Pall*

Mall Gazette) does not hold out much hope of a speedy and moderate settlement. Sir Hercules Robinson, notwithstanding his earnest desire to bring about a peace, cannot control the action of his Ministers, who have forwarded to the Basutos an ultimatum, the terms of which will almost certainly be rejected. The war will therefore be carried on to its bitter end, and the Basutos, after a prolonged resistance, will be wiped out of the map of South Africa. It has been suggested that Sir Hercules Robinson ought to put pressure upon his Ministers, and to insist upon the immediate summoning of the Colonial Parliament. It is, however, perfectly clear that such a step would be contrary to those principles of constitutional government which we thrust upon the Cape colonists less than ten years ago. If the Cape Parliament, the meeting of which has been fixed for the 25th of March, could be at once convoked, there can be little doubt that affairs would assume a different aspect. For this very reason, however, the present Cape Ministry will do nothing to hasten its assembling. Only by a *coup d'état* could Sir Hercules Robinson ignore their wishes. And, no matter how great the emergency, a *coup d'état* is not a thing to be encouraged.

The Gaikas who inhabit the district around Frankfort and King William's Town have been British subjects for five-and-twenty years; but it is said that our recent policy has also much alienated them. These are the men on whose future relationship depends the fate of South Africa. Under his own chief in the forest, says Mr. Froude, the Kaffir is at least a man trained and disciplined; under European authority he might become as fine a specimen of manhood as an Irish or English policeman. It is to our shame that we have left him almost entirely to himself, and that even our missionaries have done little more than teach him to sing hymns. Lovedale is, however, an important testimony to the worth of missionary enterprise when it takes an industrious turn. There carpentering, waggon-making, blacksmithing, printing, book-binding, cabinet-making, and farmwork are all successfully carried on. At King William's Town young native men, trained at

Lovedale, may be found employed as writers in attorneys' offices, steadily performing their work, and with satisfaction to their employers. At Edendale the Rev. James Allison commenced a still greater work. He bought a block of land near Maritzburgh, and divided it into sections suitable to humble purchasers. These purchasers were natives; his conditions were payment for these lands by instalments, and the complete surrender of polygamy. The people are described as industrious and prosperous, they subscribe to build their own chapels, and when their numbers increase beyond what the land will fairly support, they swarm out and purchase land elsewhere. 8,000 acres are thus planted, with 2,000 inhabitants. If we are to believe the Rev. Mr. Carlyle, formerly the Presbyterian chaplain at Natal, nowhere has the missionary been more successful than in South Africa.